TELL ME A STORY

by

Jonathan London

photographs by

Sherry Shahan

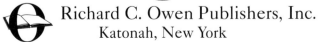
Richard C. Owen Publishers, Inc.
Katonah, New York

Meet the Author titles

Verna Aardema *A Bookworm Who Hatched*

Frank Asch *One Man Show*

Eve Bunting *Once Upon a Time*

Lois Ehlert *Under My Nose*

Jean Fritz *Surprising Myself*

Paul Goble *Hau Kola Hello Friend*

Ruth Heller *Fine Lines*

Lee Bennett Hopkins *The Writing Bug*

James Howe *Playing with Words*

Johanna Hurwitz *A Dream Come True*

Karla Kuskin *Thoughts, Pictures, and Words*

Jonathan London *Tell Me a Story*

George Ella Lyon *A Wordful Child*

Margaret Mahy *My Mysterious World*

Rafe Martin *A Storyteller's Story*

Patricia McKissack *Can You Imagine?*

Patricia Polacco *Firetalking*

Laurence Pringle *Nature! Wild and Wonderful*

Cynthia Rylant *Best Wishes*

Jean Van Leeuwen *Growing Ideas*

Jane Yolen *A Letter from Phoenix Farm*

Text copyright © 1998 by Jonathan London

Photographs copyright © 1998 by Sherry Shahan

Richard C. Owen Publishers, Inc.

PO Box 585

Katonah, New York 10536

Library of Congress Cataloging-in-Publication Data

London, Jonathan, 1947 -

 Tell me a story / by Jonathan London ; photographs by Sherry Shahan.

  p . cm . — (Meet the author)

 Summary: The author of "Froggy Gets Dressed" and other Froggy tales discusses his life, his daily activities, where he gets his ideas, and how he writes.

  ISBN 1-57274-194-5 (hardcover)

  1. London, Jonathan, 1947 - —Juvenile literature.

2. Authors, American—20th century—Biography—Juvenile literature.

3. Children's literature—Authorship— Juvenile literature.

[1. London, Jonathan, 1947 - . 2. Authors, American.]

I. Shahan, Sherry, ill. II. Title. III. Series: Meet the author (Katonah, N.Y.)

PS3562.O4874Z47 1998

813' .54—dc21

[B]   98-9374

Editorial, Art, and Production Director *Janice Boland*

Production Assistants *Donna Parsons* and *Marc Caroul*

Color separations by Leo P. Callahan Inc., Binghamton, NY

Printed in the United States of America

9 8 7 6 5 4 3 2 1

For Maureen, Aaron, and Sean,
with love

When I was little, I lived in Minnesota.
On winter mornings I'd run outside
to play in the snow.
"Johhhnnnyyy!" my mom would yell.
"Wha - a - a - t?" I'd answer.
"You have to get dressed!"

Years later, I became a dad.
My wife Maureen and I
would bundle up our young sons,
Aaron and Sean, so we could play
with them in the snow.
To me, they looked like fat little frogs.
So when they said, "Tell me a story, Daddy,"
I told them about a frog who had trouble
getting bundled up to play in the snow.
And *Froggy Gets Dressed*
became the first book in my series of Froggy tales.

I didn't always want to be a writer.
When my older brother and I were boys
our dad was an officer in the Navy.
We moved every two or three years.

I was born in Brooklyn, New York,
but we lived in New Jersey, Minnesota, Virginia,
Illinois, and Puerto Rico before we settled
in California when I was fourteen.
When I was in elementary school
I wanted to be a professional baseball player.
Later I wanted to be in the Navy like my dad.
And after that I wanted to be a history teacher.
But while I was in college I started writing poetry
and I found out that I loved to write.
After college, I joined a dance company.
I also traveled all around the world.
But guess what? I never stopped writing.
I wrote poems and short stories.
They were published in magazines.

For twenty years I wrote for no money.
Like the saxophone player in my book *Hip Cat*,
I was paid in "peanuts."
It wasn't until my kids asked me
to tell them stories and I wrote them down
that I started to make a living as a writer.

Now, I want you to wake up with me
on a typical day.
I'm a dad, so I have to help get my kids to school.

Then, every morning, Maureen and I take a long walk
with our dog Keeper. We usually walk
about four miles along Willowside Creek,
near our home in Sonoma County, California.
Here we see egrets, blue herons, turtles, frogs,
mink, deer, and sometimes even a family
of red foxes.

Around 10:00 a.m., I collect the mail from
the post office. Then I return home to work.

I work for about four hours in my writing room.
I read my mail, talk to my agent and my editors
on the phone, and work on my latest story.
I say "work," but to me it's fun.
I love writing for children.

Sometimes I concentrate so hard
that I start to shiver. And sometimes
I forget to stop and eat lunch.

My writing room is tiny. It's packed with books,
my desk, files, and my word processor.
But when I'm writing, it becomes my whole world!

I imagine I'm with the wolves in
The Eyes of Gray Wolf, or dancing around
the world with *Little Red Monkey*.

While I write, I listen to jazz. I love the cool, jazzy rhythms. Sometimes they influence my writing. Sometimes I hop up and dance to them.

When I write I never use an outline.
I let myself be surprised by what I write.
I let my stories go wherever they want to go.

On my first draft, I write fast.
I want to get the ideas down.
I use whatever words come to me
and I make lots of mistakes.
My stories usually don't come out right
the first time. I have to write
and write until I get it right.
That's called revising.

For me, revising is the hardest part of writing.
I try to choose the best words — words that are
fun to say, like "yikes!" or "fiddlesticks!"
I write musically, listening to the sounds and
rhythms of what I write.
I read my stories out loud to hear how they sound.

Often, I read or show them to my wife, and to my children and their friends.
They tell me if they like my story or not.
They are my first editors.

I'm always being asked by children, "Where do you get your ideas?"
I get them from my experiences and from my imagination.

Usually the experience I remember is small, about the size of a dime.

But my imagination is as big as a PIZZA!

We all have experiences — things that have happened to us. And we all have imaginations. So we all can make up our own stories.

I keep an idea file
so I always have
something to write
about. When I get
an idea — often in
that dreamy state
between sleeping
and waking —
I write it down on
whatever is handy:
a scrap of paper, an
envelope.

Then I file it away until I have a quiet time
to work on it.
I wrote the first draft of *Into This Night We Are Rising*
on an envelope.

And yes, even after having over fifty books
accepted for publication, I still get rejections.
But do you think I give up when that happens?
No, I don't! If I still love the story,
I keep trying until a publisher accepts it.
Froggy Gets Dressed was rejected a dozen times
before it was published.

After writing for about four hours,
I like to drive to town and go to the bookstore.
Guess what section I go to? The children's section!
I like to look at the new books at the store.
Sometimes one of the new books is mine.

Then I go to the library and do research.

If I'm writing about wolves and bears,
I read all I can about wolves and bears.
Sometimes I take home stacks of books.
I also do research by watching wild animals,
by talking to biologists and other wildlife experts,
and by asking lots of questions.

When my kids come
home from school,
I like to play with
them and their
friends. We jump
on the trampoline
in the backyard
and shoot hoops.

My kids are inspirations for my books.
They are a lot like Froggy.
One time Sean was playing soccer.
It was an important game, the City Cup
Tournament. He wasn't the goalie, but he
accidentally caught the ball in front of the goal.
"Oops!" he said, just like Froggy.
So now I'm working on a book called
Froggy Plays Soccer.

As I said, I have traveled all over the world. Some of my experiences have led me to write books.

Ali, Child of the Desert was inspired by a camel trip I took across the Sahara Desert in North Africa.

I like to go white-water rafting on wild rivers.
One time Aaron and I spent a week white-water
rafting on the Green River in Desolation Canyon,
Utah. Aaron kept a great journal of our adventure.
It became the inspiration for a chapter book
that we're working on together called *Desolation
Canyon*. It's based on our experience, but you can
bet we're using a whole lot of imagination.

I'd like to go on some more
but I forgot to eat lunch.
Then I want to go outside and play with the kids.

Other Books by Jonathan London

Fireflies, Fireflies; Fire Race: How Fire Came to the People; Light My Way; Froggy's First Kiss; Froggy Goes to School; Froggy Learns to Swim; Let's Go, Froggy; Like Butter on Pancakes; Red Wolf Country; Voices of the Wild; What Newt Could Do for Turtle

About the Photographer

Sherry Shahan is a photojournalist. She travels all over the world with her camera taking pictures of interesting people, animals, and events. Sherry is also an author and has written many books, both fiction and nonfiction. She wrote *A Coat Full of Bubbles, The Changing Caterpillar,* and *The Hungry Sea Star* for Richard C. Owen Publishers, Inc. Sherry wore this hat when she was on assignment in Alaska working on a book about dog sled racing and the Junior Iditarod.

Acknowledgments

Photographs on pages 4, 5, 6, 29, and 30 courtesy of Jonathan London. Illustration on page 5 from *Froggy Gets Dressed* by Jonathan London, illustrated by Frank Remkiewcz. Copyright © 1992 by Frank Remkiewcz, illustrations. Used by permission of Viking Penguin, a division of Penguin Books USA Inc. Illustration on page 8 from *Hip Cat* by Jonathan London, illustrated by Woodleigh Hubbard. Illustrations copyright © 1993 by Woodleigh Hubbard. Used by permission of Chronicle Books. Illustration on page 14 from *The Eyes of Gray Wolf* by Jonathan London, illustrated by John Van Zyle. Illustrations copyright © 1993 by John Van Zyle. Used by permission of Chronicle Books. Illustration on page 15 from *Little Red Monkey* by Jonathan London, illustrated by Frank Remkiewcz. Copyright © 1997 by Frank Remkiewcz, illustrations. Used by permission of Dutton Children's Books, a division of Penguin Books USA Inc. Illustration on page 23 from *Into This Night We Are Rising* by Jonathan London, illustrated by G. Brian Karas. Copyright © 1993 by G. Brian Karas, illustrations. Used by permission of Viking Penguin, a division of Penguin Books USA Inc. Illustration on page 29 from *Ali, Child of the Desert* by Jonathan London, illustrated by Ted Lewin. Illustrations copyright © 1997 by Ted Lewin. By permission of Lothrop, Lee & Shepard Books, a division of William Morrow & Company Inc.